The Book on Making It as a Broker

The Book on Making It as a Broker

How to Double Production in 12 Months

Scott Peppard

ISBN: 978-1-4525-5058-9 (sc)
ISBN: 978-1-4525-5057-2 (e)

Balboa Press books may be ordered through booksellers or by contacting:

Balboa Press
A Division of Hay House
1663 Liberty Drive
Bloomington, IN 47403
www.balboapress.com
1-(877) 407-4847

Printed in the United States of America

Balboa Press rev. date: 12/02/2013

One of the most helpful and inspiring books on salesmanship that I have ever read.

Mike Collier
Author & world-renowned business coach
Los Angeles

Scott provides thoughtful, practical, relevant and timely investment ideas to some of the most accomplished financial advisors in the country. Scott's presentations were riveting and created immediate action.

Mike Rutler
Business Development Officer
Washington D.C.

This book will help anyone who wants to be successful in sales and/or starting a business.

Dan Swallow
Financial Product Wholesaler
Philadelphia

Scott's talents as a public speaker are only surpassed by his motivational skills, which are superb."

Stephen Barbera
Financial Advisor
Manhattan

My production increased significantly in one month from Scott's ideas!

Will Puvogel
Financial Advisor
New York

Scott's instruction is the best we've ever seen in terms of subject matter, delivery and ultimately broker feedback.

Kevin Grimm
Director of Sales
Manhattan

Scott's material and presentation style energizes his listeners.

Neal Lee
Financial Product Wholesaler
Washington D.C.

My business grew significantly after incorporating Scott's ideas.

Mark J. Sklar
Media PA

Scott's meeting was the best I've ever attended!

Stefano Airo
Financial Advisor
New York

Scott's has helped me raise millions.

Charlie Lawrence
Productivity Consultant
New Jersey

Dedication

To all of the "teachers" in my life-past, present and future.

Secondarily, I consecrate this book to those that have told me "NO" over the years.

Foreword

Written by Raymond Aaron

After seeing the amazing effect Scott had on people, I urged him to write a book, so he could share his experiences, techniques and philosophy of selling. In business, as in life, one needs to master two things: communication and relationships. This mastery will be apparent after reading just a few chapters of this book.

When Scott first asked me to write the foreword to *The Book on Making it as a Broker*, I was grateful for the opportunity. We met in August 2011 at a marketing course I was conducting, not too far from Times Square. Scott clearly stood out, as he was not the garden-variety seminar attendee. He already owned a successful company that was generating sales and cash flow. However, as Scott knew, in order to continue prospering in his business, he needed exposure to transformational ideas and concepts. Scott wanted to get better, and did, by attending my seminar. Although I would not consider Scott a perfectionist, (which can often divert one from reaching their goals), he was a driver for excellence.

Scott's insight and quick wit radiate throughout the book. Scott challenges many of the conventional methods (i.e., contact, qualification, closing) for gaining more business. He has resuscitated an unpopular topic in sales training – prospecting - and given it new life with spirit and excitement. The book avoids clichés and hollowed expressions, and instead offers a blueprint of cutting edge strategies to help double your business.

If you want to unstick your career or company, this book will be an eye-opener. The first epiphany is that doubling activity does not double your income. You'll discover why working harder is not scalable and more sales calls will not equate to more dollars. Competing with others on the playing field of transactional activity is idiotic. Instead, learn Scott's innovative ideas and tactics to lap and leap the competition.

You'll find Scott's approach to be counter intuitive but also full of common sense. He is a tactician and advances with methods that have been effective in his own sales work.

The massive download of information available in today's world requires best how position your product and grab one's attention. At the risk of sounding blasphemous, getting another professional credential will not do it. In marketing, it's not what you know or whom you know, but who knows you that counts. You're better off becoming a student, not of your market, but of this book.

The best teachers are also the best students…and Scott is both the former and latter. His book is not an ordinary work. It's extraordinary.

Raymond Aaron
NY Times Best-Selling Author
www.MillionaireBusinessBootcamp.com

Acknowledgements

Writing a book is a universal effort, and as such, I would like to thank my wife, Donna-without your input, love, affection, patience (with minimal eye-rolling) and belief in me this book would never have come to fruition.

Gracias to my business coaches, Mike Collier and Raymond Aaron-amigos, you both continue to lead me by the example you set.

And amen Kathleen Rutler, my editor, for your astute observations, recommendations and eagle eye.

Introduction

In the early spring of 2005 I had an interview scheduled with Scott Peppard. I knew nothing of Scott other than he was ex-Merrill. At the time, I was heading a fast-growing sales team in a turbo-charged young financial services company. The minute I met Scott that day I recall saying two things: 1. This guy is different; and 2. He not only understands the advisory business, he understands the human spirit. It was one of my better hires.

Scott had such a quiet confidence about him that was contagious. I saw this time and time again in our sales and product training meetings where, Scott would seemingly have just heard a new portfolio managers /asset class story and get up minutes later to present it flawlessly to his peers. Little did I know, he had already spent hour after hour in preparation. It became clear to me that success did not come to Scott without tireless preparation.

In addition, I saw in Scott a love and passion not just for the business, but also, more importantly, for the people in the business. That too was contagious. This quiet confidence turned into active mentoring and teaching, not only to our team but also for countless numbers of financial advisers caught in his wake.

When Scott left our firm for a "more risky" endeavor, I laughed, although a temporary hardship, and wished him well because I knew he was fulfilling the entrepreneurial spirit inside him and quit frankly knew, he needed to fly more freely. Some questioned his sanity, I questioned their free-market spirit and their desire to grow and be challenged. I knew that's what Scott was doing.

What will you learn from this book?

1. Perspective. So often our willingness to change simply requires a new perspective, a different viewpoint. You will get it here.
2. That good deeds and good work go hand in hand. If you want to change the culture you are in, you must first change your own.
3. That if you are doing business like everyone else, you are doing it wrong; the masses are not extraordinary.

If you read this book you will be happier, more productive and more successful. Period.

Tony DiLeonardi
Author of: ***The $14 Trillion Woman***
Oct. 2013

Preface

Vincent: "This is my job, Eddie."

Fast Eddie Felson: "You think so? That's funny. I don't think so. I think it's your problem."

The Color of Money 1986

***"All the greats, to a man, were student of human moves."* -Fast Eddie Felson**
The Color of Money 1986

***"...if you're too careful, your whole life can be a grind."* -Matt Damon**
from the movie Rounders

Prior to the turn of the century, most Americans worked for themselves; the remaining were employed in an apprentice capacity to learn a trade that would ultimately lead to self employment. People were not taught how to pucker up to a boss, they were shown in practical ways how to make things happen.

In 1900, the United States underwent an industrialized revolution. As a direct result, big business was formed. Government entities started into motion. People were moving away from a largely agrarian society towards one where groups of people now worked together for the benefit of someone else-an owner-"the boss".

What did these institutions require? Salaried employees will to exchange their freedom for a steady paycheck; people whose only dreams were to put food on the table and to just "get by".

People began to leave the fields to work for a guaranteed paycheck and a minimal standard of living. They resigned themselves to perform largely unskilled tasks, letting the owners call all of the shots.

Although our society has become more cultured, and employees more skilled the fact is that salaried employees are not in any way free and will always have to answer to someone else or be fired.

Salaried folks forgo their dreams, willing to dedicate the best years of their lives promoting someone else's. "This is as good as it's going to get", they say while they "bite the bullet". "We broke, but we happy."

Day after day, week after week, year after year and all of a sudden, life is over. And how was it spent-punching a clock, making someone else rich?

98% of our population is controlled by time and money. 60% of the wives in this country work outside of the home and it is not because they are bored. Statistics show that out of every 100 working people, 36 will be dead before they see the age of 65. The major cause is a heart attack caused by the stress, strain and anxiety trying to make a five dollar bill go where a fifty is needed. One cannot be happy when day to day living expenses are all-consuming. Not only is health affected but relationships suffer as well: 90% of all marital arguments are over a lack of money.

This book is about putting the free back in free enterprise. A broker, agent, commissioned salesman/advisor is one of the few remaining vehicles where the individual person can call the shots. This book has been penned to honor the noblest of all professions: sales.

From the day that we were born we have been taught that sales is not a good thing, the image of the travelling salesman, the used-car salesman, the door-to-door salesman has tainted the credibility of the trade.

However, the top earners in the United States are salespeople.

When I first got into the business, I could not afford my house or my doctor. Now I make more than my doctor and I have a bigger house. I sell the service of helping people make decisions and you can too. I help people make decisions that are good for them; and that decision might be to decline my offering.

The concepts presented in **Making it as a Broker** are based on the experiences of successful business owners. These principles are timeless and relevant to building your brokerage business. This treatise is for the broker, salesman, advisor and agent in any industry who is interested in transforming his practice. I will lay a foundation for helping you to build a business. Making it as a Broker will serve as a road map to doubling production in half the time and with half the effort.

The information you are about to be exposed to is the result of studying successful people for thirty years; wisdom from "the ages" bringing to light the methodology of commanding huge incomes in all market cycles.

Some techniques come from my working days at Merrill Lynch, McDonald's Corporation and selling freight space in Port Newark. The name of your company or product is incidental. We are in the business of people-methods are many and will change; principles are few and never do.

The concepts I put before you will revolutionize your business as long as you are ready to read and ponder. The beautiful thing about being in a free society is that you do not have to read or listen to anyone or anything. On the other hand, if you are busted, if money or the lack of money is controlling you, if you are "sick and tired of being sick and tired", then read on. Simply working harder, keeping your head down, ear to the ground, nose to the grindstone and shoulder to the wheel is not scalable.

Take a look around your community. Why are septuagenarians serving McMuffins to adolescents? Ask any seventy-year old in a retail position why he is shilling burgers or straightening out racks instead of lounging in his Golden Years. Interview them, I have. At one time, most of them had "good" jobs and their purchasing power was greater than yours-back then earners were paid with hard cash, unlike today's 'fiat' money.

A lot of people think that they are doing well financially, but that depends on the comparison. What are your standards and how do they stack up against friends, family and acquaintances? Who is broke and who is considered to being doing well? Where do you think you fit? What about raising the bar?

Every successful person is continuously raising the bar. Successful people never level off-they keep going. They do not reach a plateau and sit back and say they are done. Less ambitious folks may look at strivers, shake their heads sadly and say mockingly "Are you never satisfied?" Which of the two groups has earned complete and total financial freedom? What about living life the way you want to instead of being controlled by time and money? If someone else signs your paycheck, you are being paid the least amount it would cost to replace you.

Do what economics in America is based on: free enterprise. Christopher Columbus and other early explorers did not set sail to get a job. The Pilgrims did not come here solely for religious tolerance. Immigrants throughout history did not come here to be slaves. They all ventured out with dreams of freedom and financial gain; the opportunity to live in the land of opportunity and an economic system developed by Adam Smith.

Every man who works for someone else dreams about going out on their own. After ten years of spinning their wheels in the rut system, many decide to take the leap and do something solo. Many also step right "out of the frying pan and into the fire." The deck is stacked against small business because most are under-capitalized. More significantly, many small business owners lack direction and knowledge.

Five years ago I went from a traditional salaried position to full commission and I haven't looked back. No other business has a lower start-up cost with a higher potential income than that of a broker. This book will give you the knowledge to make it on your own, to make it as a broker.

"By prevailing over all obstacles and distractions, one may unfailingly arrive at his chosen goal or destination."-Christopher Columbus

Making it as a Broker by Scott Peppard

Excerpts from the book

"If you want to grow your business, grow yourself. What is your dream? Without a dream, a goal, a reason or a purpose, it's not going to work. Dreams are motivators and without them, chances of succeeding are very slim. It is good to identify the reason to set goals for yourself so that you will not look backwards, but move ahead with all the energy and conviction of a great explorer. Dreams inspire conscious decisions to move ahead."

"Sometimes we don't know what it takes to succeed-every single success story of the people mentioned in Chapter Two follows the same pattern of dream-struggle-victory. What started as a dream became an almost tunnel-vision-like struggle, resulting in a phenomenal victory. None of the self-made millionaires and billionaires gave up and remained optimistic that their visions would come to fruition, no matter what it took."

"You can have anything you want. If you can dream it, you can make it happen."

"Success is a decision."

"The name of your company or product is incidental. We are in the business of people-methods are many and will change, principles are few and never do."

Contents

Chapter One

GET UNSTUCK

Is your territory stuck? Doubling activity will not double your income. Working harder is not scalable - don't equate more sales calls to more dollars. Competing with other salespeople on the playing field of transactional activity is idiotic. Learn to lap and leap by becoming the authority in your industry vis-à-vis educational marketing.

At the risk of sounding blasphemous, getting another finance credential will NOT increase Box 1 of your W-2. It doesn't matter what you know or who you know, but who knows you that counts. You're better off becoming a student, not of the markets, but of marketing and branding.

Sad but true, people do judge a book by its cover. Your network is your net-worth and knowing more about kurtosis or Sharpe ratios will increase neither. So if your production has plateaued, get unstuck by thinking not like a salesperson, but a marketer. Sales is when you call them; marketing is when they call you. With good niche marketing, sales are easy. Because the cornerstone of marketing is education, begin introducing novel and innovative ideas to your prospects.

How do you find valuable strategies to share? Read books on marketing and enroll in the affiliated seminar. Attend trade associations OUTSIDE your industry and become a conceptual learner. Observe or extract their systems, procedures, processes and thinking. That is, take filaments (advertising, writing copy, sales literature, etc.) from non-related industries, combine into hybrids and show prospects how to import and implement into their business. Examples may include:

- Referral techniques Realtors use (to gain listings) may be more effective than the status quo employed by your industry.
- Principles revealed at Ritz-Carlton's Leadership Center may help strengthen client longevity. The possibilities are endless.

Your client's business is a pretty good indicator of yours and the secondary benefit of associating with outside industries is learning about your clients' clients. Share a profitable idea picked up and you become not only memorable, but also indispensable. That's the goal: to be the de facto trusted advisor by being perceived as the problem solver/solution finder. This is accomplished through helping your people optimize their systems, practices and procedures. Here are two ideas I picked up attending business seminars unrelated to the financial services industry:

1. When emailing clients or prospects, put their name in the subject line - they are more apt to read it. Dale Carnegie's advice is as true today as it was more than 80 years ago: "a person's name is the sweetest, most important and recognizable sound in any language." If there's an attachment (PDF, word doc, etc.), save it in the recipient's name.
2. I have always been a fan of leaving detailed voice messages for prospects and clients. It is more powerful than email and often easier to telegraph your pitch than an actual conversation. Plus you can professionally bypass any gatekeepers. The problem is voicemail stamina - after five dials, enthusiasm begins to wane. The solution? Digitally record your pitch and play it back on each of your prospect's voicemail. By scripting a well-crafted message, you can duplicate your zeal over and over again - you've just captured lightning in a bottle!

If you want to make inroad and develop relationships quickly, book broadcast meetings. Effective speaking is a short cut to distinction - when you present in public, people automatically overate your skills, talent and intelligence. Weighting branch meetings over individual sales calls doubled my income in one year.

Lunch presentations don't work because the garden-variety salesperson rolls in at 11:55AM. The ceremony is typically done with no stage setting (i.e., apropos lighting, chair arrangement, air temp, email/voicemail invites, endorsements, scripted announcement, etc.) Then to make a banal situation grave, the topic is always a financial product, never the client. People don't want your stuff, they want profit - so stop pitching product. It's no mystery lunch meetings have 20% attendance rates.

Make the thesis of your next on a novel business practice you discovered while mining outside the industry. Lunch meetings are a piece of theatre and if orchestrated correctly, can transform your production. Your role is to educate on how to generate referrals and write bigger/better business, not simply to "bring in" assets. If you share something of value, it comes back to you: the law of reciprocity is irrefutable and biblical. Some call it educational marketing, I call it a cosmic bribe and math of the Universe. So don't be surprised when your clients offer to pick up the tab at your next lunch meeting. Mission accomplished - you're now branded as the authority.

Chapter Two

ALL MASTERS START OUT AS DISASTERS

***"You are never too old to set another goal or to dream a new dream."*-C.S. Lewis, author**

Get Rich Quick Schemes

I tried everything. I was one of those guys who watched cable TV every night looking for my fortune.

"I know it's going to be on Channel 39, I just know it," I would say to myself.

The Real Estate No Money Down Programs-I ordered them all-the cassette tapes, the CD's, the bonus cassettes and the bonus CD's. I tuned into every get-rich-quick seminar, subscribed to all of the supporting newsletters and up-dated all programs via the Internet and the mail. I was on the multi-level marketing bandwagon. My home-office was piled from floor to ceiling with sure-fire infomercial campaigns. You name it, I dabbled in it.

Education

I tried going back to school, you know-when all else fails get an advanced degree-you can't have too much education, right? I did what the system in America taught me to do, to be educated but broke. We were taught to get a good education, gain real-life experience and exchange it for a decent salary-the American Dream right?

Experience

As per instruction, I went out and got a "good job"-one that looked like it spelled success. A Global Brokerage Firm with a prestigious name. In no time at all, I earned a fancy title; I got up every day and did what I was programmed to do-doing the same thing day in and day out for over eighteen years. I was climbing the Corporate Ladder of Success, and was called in one day a year by the Head Honcho (who also got called in annually by his Head Honcho, who got called in by HIS Head Honcho and so on).

"Scott, you're doing a tremendous job for us and we really appreciate it!"

"We want you to know that you've given us a fantastic effort,(my spirits soar) but (here comes corporate double-talk) you've got to understand it's been a difficult year for the firm as a whole. We can only give you 3% to recognize your individual efforts (hopes are dashed here)."

"You may not realize it when it happens, but a kick in the teeth might be the best thing in the world for you." –Walt Disney

The problem was (and still is), that the real rate of inflation is 7% per annum, so before I even left his office, I was in the hole by 4%. The raise also moved me up into the next tax bracket-**what inflation missed, Uncle Sam grabbed and I became a two-time loser.**

But I did get a handshake, a smile and the impressive new title of Vice President. I looked good, smelled good as was going to be even broker than when I woke up that morning!

False Hopes and Unrealized Dreams

Still, I wanted people to think I was doing well, heck, I wanted to think I was doing well. After all, I was a highly educated professional. I looked good in a suit, but the reality was that I was living from check to check. I compared myself to other struggling salaried executives-we were all in the same boat-broke and unhappy, but smiling on the outside to keep up appearances.

My wife and I would regularly run out of money before we ran out of month. The paycheck I received every other Thursday was spent before Friday! I can remember getting paid by the cashier, riding in the elevator of the fanciest, most prestigious office in New Jersey to the ground floor, walking three blocks to the teller at the bank and kissing it goodbye. I was simply covering checks written three days prior.

But I looked good, smelled good and was prepared to run on the treadmill to retirement. Isn't that what you did?

Behind the scenes and often stilted smiles, we were living a life of quiet desperation. I wanted more for my family, but did not have the means to do so. We were earning barely enough to get by, but kept asking ourselves the classic question: Isn't there more to life than this? I felt like a hamster in a cage, running and running in a circle without clearly defined goals, no beginning or end in sight, just repetitious motion for no reward. And yet, some would define our lives as successful.

Strip away all of the superficial trimmings and try this out to determine your level of success: look at your bank balance. There it is in black and white. Financial health can be measured simply by a growing bank balance-bringing home more than you need now to secure a better life in the future. Broke people traditionally spend about 10% more than they make. We were broke alright.

Broke people live for the moment and also for their tax returns and I speak from a position of experience. Most wealthy people do not file their taxes until the night before they are due, keeping their money in interest-bearing accounts until the very last minute. They are not going to give the government even one penny before they absolutely have to. I used to file my tax return by January 31st, hounding the office manager for my W2 before the fifteenth in order to put a dent on my debts. No matter what my New Year's resolutions were, each year I was in the same desperate position.

My wife Donna and I reached a breaking point-we owned car that wouldn't start on a cold day, a 'pre-owned' Nova that leaked oil out as fast as I could put it in. We wanted, in fact needed a new car, but were reduced to two and three times pre-owned-used.

I was making $55,000 (gross income) back then and proudly said to my wife: "You can get the used Chrysler of your choice," making our own donation to the country's carbon emission problem.

That's where we were after 15 years together. I had promised her the moon the night we were married and now the closest we got to it was a view of it through the window on a clear night. Worse yet, Donna was wondering why I was less and less excited about getting up for work on Monday mornings than I used to be.

I was 40 years old and burned out.

Eureka!

***"There are two types of pain in this world: pain that hurts you and pain that changes you."*- Anonymous**

It was time to make a move.

I was sick and tired of being sick and tired (and broke). I needed to make a change. But when, what and how? I sat up in bed one Monday morning and said enough! No more whining! No more oil-eating bombers parked in the driveway. No more living from paycheck to paycheck and whistling in the wind. I, actually my wife, was mad as hell and not going to take it anymore.

If you want to change some things in your life, you have to change some things in your life. Sounds like double-talk doesn't it? Some feel-good, self-help rhetoric?

***"What the mind can conceive and believe, it can achieve."*-Napoleon Hill**

We all have fears, things to overcome, challenges of some sort. But those with a strong dream set goals for themselves and if they want something bad enough, they will work hard to achieve those goals. Many naysayers will discourage young hopefuls by citing statistics for success, but when you know who you are and what you want, you can achieve anything.

Most people focus on the work, on a job and as a result have a tough time. In the beginning, I did not have a dream, other than of taking my bosses' job as soon as possible. I did not have a dream but instead, a nightmare. I didn't necessarily want material things like a nicer car, bigger house or a great vacation. I wanted freedom and financial independence. I did not want to spend my life working to make someone else free.

It was time to make a move. I was prepared to go to the next level and be compensated in direct proportion to my efforts. Two years ago, I quit a $325,000 per year job, with benefits, to pursue my dream of independent business ownership. Was it scary? You bet. My thinking was, I'd rather make $100,000 and be free than $300,000 of indentured servitude.

Don't Listen to Your Inner or Outer Critics

The president of the company I left thought I was nuts for giving up a sure thing, security, a solid base. Friends looked at me sideways, shaking their heads critically. One acquaintance chastised me vehemently for jeopardizing my family by giving up what appeared to be a great career in a prestigious firm. How could I walk away from a company with a proven track record, a secure job in a scary economic time and launch myself into uncertainty-without benefits no less!

Freedom was my initial reason for leaving but the many criticisms and even a few tongue lashings made me more determined than ever to prove people wrong. I was starting over at 40, but in two years time I would become successful as my own boss while the doubters and naysayers remained stagnated where they were-still working for someone else's benefit.

It wasn't easy, but at 40, I felt as though I walked into the land of the living. I would never again be controlled by a person, time or money. I surrounded myself with successful and positive people and work my own business plan.

Five years ago I was broke, drove a used Jeep and lived in a crappy rental apartment next to a strip joint. Today my wife drives a Porsche and depending on my mood, I take the Volvo or the BMW. We live in beautiful, cultured Princeton, New Jersey. I am now a free person at 47 years old, living in the top 1% income bracket. I haven't been controlled by anyone since 2010. Instead of rolling over, I rolled out.

I did my time folks, I played the game and then broke free, putting to use everything I had learned in the first 40 years. I am not a big shot, do not have any fancy titles nor can I point to prestigious plaques on an ostentatious office wall. But I will compare lifestyles any day.

A salaried position will always interfere with your true worth.

The need for a salary or to be paid hourly comes with a trade-off-the loss of financial and often personal freedom. It is nearly impossible to chase freedom and have the security of employment. Wealthy people choose to be compensated based on results. Broke people want to be paid on time. Those who need guaranteed income via a company check fear that working for themselves will not provide an ample living for their families.

I did not see any salaried people living the way I wanted to live; tethered to a desk groveling for 3% raises. I did not want to live in a fear and scarcity-based way. Commissioned sales people on the other hand seemed to be living the dream. Selling is the world's oldest profession and if you are good, you can make a fortune.

> ***"Going to work for a large company is like getting on a train. Are you going 60mph or is the train going 60mph while you are sitting still."*** **–J. Paul Getty, billionaire oilman**

Most wealthy people own their own businesses, either partially or outright. Their income is from business profit whether it is commissioned sales, stock options or a percentage of the take- not time spent punching a clock. Wealthy people look for opportunities, broke people look for a raise.

My own father, a real estate entrepreneur, tended to be conservative and often overly protective; it was natural for him to promote a secure existence. He kept telling me to get a good government job with a pension and benefits. Conversely, I advise my kids to make sure they are paid on percentages.

The path to sales is not always rosy-being a broker, if done haphazardly, can become an expensive hobby. For some, it is a dignified road to starvation. There is no middle class, you either make it or you don't.

Career or Job (Jump Out of Bed or Just Over Broke)

Is it possible to make a six-figure, portable, somewhat passive income working 9-5? The 11th Commandment should read 'Though Shalt Not Kid Thyself'. Oftentimes we look at others and think they have it all together, that their lives are easy. When we see success, some may assume that wealthy people were born that way, made connections in the Ivies or had an impressive inheritance. However, upon further investigation, you will find that high achievers went through a lot of ups and downs to get where they are. We often see the fruits but not the labor. Every successful person I interviewed survived incredible set-backs. Winners realize that some failure is inevitable and learn from it; losers give up.

"You don't learn to walk by following rules. You learn by doing and falling over."
–Richard Branson, billionaire founder of Virgin Airlines and Virgin Music

What is the Gestalt of the minds of the "intrepid set", those in the top 3% income bracket? What is the difference between how these guys tick and the other 97% who often fail to live up to their financial potential? Are there universal principles that highly commissioned agents have for successes and cycle-proof incomes?

General George S. Patton once said success is defined by how high you bounce after hitting bottom. You are hit with rejection and may ask yourself why you are doing this. Refocus. There will always be good and bad things in your life.

Better Not Bitter

When I worked for Merrill, I was continually passed over for commissioned sales positions. One interview came to an abrupt halt when the interviewer said the venue was now changing into a course on what and what not to do during an interview! I was humiliated, but rather than getting bitter, I got better. I honed my skills and continued to seek other opportunities.

Failure tempers the mettle of which you are composed. Many who succeed in life get off to a bad start and pass through many heart-breaking struggles before they arrive. Top brokers in their industry have many more no's than yeses. The fork in the road of success always comes at the point of crisis and misfortune. Here is where you get introduced to your authentic self.

Thomas Alva Edison quit formal schooling after his teacher labeled him "addled". He later became a tramp telegraph operator before he "found" himself and became one of the most important inventors of his time.

***"If we all did the things we are capable of, we would astound ourselves."* –Thomas Alva Edison, inventor/scientist**

Think about your past successes-I'll bet they came one step beyond the point of which defeat had almost over-taken you.

Once I finally landed a commissioned position, I had to get past inevitable initial rejections. I had to learn was that just talking with a client wouldn't guarantee a career-it was a numbers game. I had to sift through a hundred no's to get to the golden yes.

Try this fun exercise: Take a roll of two-ply bath tissue and write a person's name on each sheet that rejected your unique selling proposition. Each time you get a no, tear, toss and go, "later!" By the time you are done, you will be making $100,000.

Opportunity makes its appearance in a different form and is often disguised as rejection. Hope always comes from an entirely unexpected source.

The book ***Think & Grow Rich*** by Napoleon Hill should be required reading for all who desire to succeed in this profession as it succinctly details vehicle, mission and vision. No time to read? Books are the source of invaluable information not taught in school. Merrill Lynch's number one producer claimed that it was this book that was at the heart of the turning point of his practice.

Penned in the depths of the Great Depression, Hill interviewed 20,000 people over the course of twenty years. He sat for hours with giants like George Eastman, William Wrigley, Marshall Field, JD Rockefeller, FW Woolworth, Edward A. Filene, Henry Ford, Thomas Edison and Charlie Schwab. Interestingly enough, these wealthy individuals did not come from money, lacked family influence and had little formal education.

Every success story was the same: dream/struggle/victory-in that order. Over and over again, Hill revealed stories of successful people who had been through what you may be going through and then some.

I used to believe that triumph or victory after defeat was a Sunday school lesson-the soft-value kind of Pollyanna-thinking; a way to make people feel better about losing. I have since learned that broke people get mad easily and that the size of a man may be best determined by the size of the things that make him mad enough to do something about them.

After reading (and listening to the audio) of Hill's book countless times, I believe "the secret" to financial success is that in *every coincidence, delay, disturbance, inconvenience, mistake, oversight, discouragement, obstacle, problem, frustration, struggle, opposition, argument, fight, embarrassment, degradation, depreciation, put down, set up, set back, regret, penalty, humiliation, trip up, double cross, disappointment, remorse, adversity, crisis, defeat, misfortune, failure and tragic experience lies hidden success, hope, opportunity, blessing, lesson, advantage and ultimate victory.* But it is disguised and you must train your eyes, mind, heart, gut and attitude to recognize it.

If you put money on a vertical scale and attitude on a horizontal scale with a negative attitude to the left and positive to the right, you will find people's finances in direct proportion to their attitude. The more positive their attitude, the more money they make; the more negative or lower self-image, the less income.

"If you fell down yesterday, stand up today. The crisis of today is the joke of tomorrow." –
H.G. Wells, author of science fiction

Chapter Three

HOW A FORMAL EDUCATION MIGHT MAKE YOU BROKE

"Drop out of school before your mind rots from our mediocre educational system." – Frank Zappa

***"Failure in school does not mean failure in life."* –Stephen J. Cannell, author, Emmy award-winning TV producer, dyslexic**

Our antiquated school system was formed around the turn of the century. America is the greatest country in the world, yet it does not teach its children its own system of economics. People have been taught by a school system that is 110 years old how to get a good education, experience and knowledge on how to go out and get a good job, almost guaranteeing them the right to fail. THE MORE EDUCATION ONE HAS, THE BIGGER ONE'S MONEY PROBLEMS.

Knowledge is not power. Applied, specialized knowledge is power. Generalized education and market value are an inverse relationship. Sound countercultural? I used to think that the more educated one becomes, the wealthier they became.

Growing up, I had a wide circle of friends: jocks, gear heads, surfers, dopers, brainiacs, and farm kids. Fast forward twenty-five years-my most successful friend was a marginal student. This gentleman barely made it through high school and dropped out of community college after attending for one day. Today he is a wealthy business owner and real estate entrepreneur. My least financially successful friend earned straight A's and is currently a University professor.

***"It is strange the way the ignorant and inexperienced so often and so undeservedly succeed when the informed and the experienced fail."* – Mark Twain, newspaper reporter, riverboat pilot, humorist, novelist, prospector**

Money is not the only ingredient to success, neither is poverty. Money won't buy you happiness, but neither will being busted. If you want to succeed, you have to possess what teachers criticized you for in school-a dream. God said in Proverbs "a man without vision shall perish." The word 'shall' is not to be taken lightly. It does not mean possibly, might or ought to perish. It means will.

In my six years of college, I received only one hour of instruction from anybody that had done what they were teaching. If the professor had not "practiced what he preached" then what gave him credibility? I wanted to learn what was effective in the real world, not what might work on paper.

Money will control you if you never learn how to control it-a topic never taught in school.

The sad part about education is that you have been taught how to fail. Upon graduation, some students may sign their life away on a contractual obligation as a salaried employee; and not necessarily a successful one. A recent Forbes article headlined the statistic that 75% of college students return home to live with their parents after graduation. A Bloomberg survey found that those who earned a master's degree typically earn one third less than those holding a bachelor's.

Although shocking and countercultural, there is a point at which a college education becomes over-valued. Unless of course your only goal in life is to have a job. That's the scam.

Ever hear the expression "A" students wind up teaching and "B" students work for "C" students?

It is true more often than not because the person who knows how always works for the person who knows why. Attend any high school reunion, do an informal survey and the statistics will bear out. **Financial planners never ask investors for a report card.**

This is not a secret amongst the wealthy. Ever since America became an industrialized nation-the more education you receive, the worse the job you will get. Why does our sophisticated society allow one to spend money getting an education in failure?

The following is a very small sampling of those who have become wildly successful with little or no formal education. And granted, though the times have changed, it is mainly the soaring income reflected, influenced by technology and the advent of a true global economy.

"Genius is 1% inspiration and 99% perspiration."
– Thomas Alva Edison, inventor

Quit Elementary School

- Abraham Lincoln- Lawyer, U.S. President
- Christopher Columbus-Explorer, Discoverer of America
- Davy Crockett-19th-century American folk hero soldier, politician and "King of the Wild Frontier".
- Thomas Edison-The world's greatest inventor and scientist
- Patrick Henry-Founding Father, American patriot, orator and statesman.
- William Shakespeare-playwright, poet
- Clement Stone-multimillionaire insurance businessman, founder of *Success* magazine, author of a number of books on positive mental attitudes

- Mark Twain-printer, riverboat pilot, prospector, newspaper reporter, humorist, best-selling novelist
- George Washington-the Father of Our Country, first U.S. President, military commander

Eight of the 43 people who served as U.S. President never went to college.

Quit High School

- Peter Giannini-multi-millionaire, founder of Bank of America
- Anne Beiler-multi-millionaire co-founder of Auntie Anne's Pretzels, philanthropist
- Ansel Adams-world-famous photographer
- Tom Anderson-co-founder of 'Myspace'
- Richard Branson-billionaire founder of Virgin Music and Atlantic Airways
- Jack Kent Cooke-billionaire media mogul, Washington Redskins owner
- Charles Culpeper-multi-millionaire owner and CEO of Coca Cola
- Bobby Fischer-Grandmaster chess player
- W.T. Grant-multi-millionaire founder of W.T. Grant Department Store chain
- Alfred E. Smith-governor of New York and presidential candidate known for quipping that he received his FFM degree from the Fulton Fish Market in New York City

- Dave Thomas-billionaire founder of Wendy's
- H.G. Wells-science fiction author
- Frank Lloyd Wright-architect, interior designer, leader of the Prairie School of Architecture, voted as the greatest American architect of all times by the American Institute of Architects
- Orville Wright-inventor of the airplane

"I have had all the disadvantages required for success. The most important aspect of my personality as far as determining my success goes has been my questioning of conventional wisdom, doubting experts and questioning authority. While that can be painful in your relationships with parents and teachers, it is enormously useful in life." –Larry Ellison

College Drop-Outs

- Albert Einstein-scientist
- Paul Allen-billionaire founder of Microsoft, founder of Xiant Software, owner of the Seattle Seahawks and Portland Trail Blazers
- Sheldon Adelson-billionaire casino owner
- Carl Bernstein-Watergate reporter, Washington Post
- Warren Buffett-billionaire chairman of Berkshire Hathaway
- Winston Churchill-British Prime Minister, historian, artist
- Michael Dell-billionaire founder of Dell Computers

- Larry Ellison-billionaire co-founder of Oracle Software
- Shawn Fanning-developer of Napster
- Bill Gates-billionaire co-founder of Microsoft
- J.Paul Getty-billionaire oilman, world's richest man back in the day
- Steve Jobs-billionaire co-founder of Apple Computers and Pixar Animation, Disney's largest shareholder
- Joel Osteen-pastor and host of the highest rated inspirational TV show
- William Safire-columnist for the New York Times
- Steven Spielberg-billionaire movie director/ producer, co-founder of DreamWorks
- Ted Turner-billionaire founder of CNN and TBS, owner of the Atlanta Braves, philanthropist, America's largest landowner with 1.8 million acres
- Steve Wozniak-billionaire co-founder of Apple
- Mark Zuckerberg-billionaire founder of Facebook

And this is the short list! Pretty convincing class list isn't it? Proof that it is not all about the grades, diplomas, degrees or credentials; makes you wonder why a person recently laid off would scurry back to school, find another job and get right back on the employee treadmill. How do you spell masochist?

Actor John C. Reilly's view on a Job
"I mean, this totally mystifies me. Can you believe people actually accept this? It's like you work all day, people tell you what to do all day long. You know, and then on top of taking shit all day, they can fire you."

Most of us have been brought up the same way. We were told, "go to school, get good grades, get recruited by a good company and live the good life." How's that working out? Becoming a salesman did not fit into how I was taught to succeed.

The school system was not designed to instruct its pupils on how to become wealthy, let alone run a business. By and large, teachers are broke, unionized, government employees. My career instruction came from a high school guidance counselor who earned $18,000 a year. Therefore, he was qualified to teach me how to make $18,000 a year. Only someone who has done it can show me the money. No one should teach what they have not done. Have you ever met a wealthy professor? How about the professional student-types who see all of the angles in life, but don't have the mettle to play, engage and implement. They make all of the predictions, dispel all of the myths. If you don't make money on your predictions, you haven't predicted what counts.

***"There is very little difference in people, but that little makes a big difference. The little difference is attitude"* –Clement Stone, multi-millionaire founder of "Success Magazine"/author**

Chapter Four

TALK TO THE MANY TO FIND THE FEW

***"As we look ahead into the next century, leaders will be those who empower others."*- Bill Gates, billionaire founder of Microsoft**

The first step in gaining financial success is to get out of the office and meet people. Some people stay in their office bubbles, their ivory towers, claiming they could get rich anytime they wanted to, they just had to make the decision. They think they're going to stay in the office and become wealthy.

Repeat this mantra: Your network equals your worth.

Your network equals your net worth. Think about that. Start by becoming a civic and fraternal animal. Rotary, Jaycees, Lions Club, Elks, Moose, Kiwanis,

Chamber of Commerce-a few of the many organizations to get involved with for networking.

"Success is not how much you keep, but how much you give away. It will always come back to you in some way. Give to get to give away."
-Anne Beiler, co-founder of
Auntie Anne's Pretzels

If you want to make inroads and develop relationships quickly, you must be a talker, not a taker. You must get good at public speaking which will become a short cut to distinction. You can achieve more in twenty minutes presenting at networking groups than in twenty years of silent membership. Groups like the Rotary Club, which is an international organization, meet weekly and are always looking for speakers, especially those who combine philanthropy with their work. People automatically overate public speakers, giving higher marks on the speaker's skills, talents and abilities. Enthusiasm goes a long way in the memories of the listeners.

I was the shyest guy in high school. I remember a time during senior year when we had to introduce ourselves in front of the student body, parents and faculty. I walked up, looked out over a sea of faces and froze. I literally choked. It was the most embarrassing and humiliating moment of my life. I vowed that it would never happen again.

I also learned that after six years of dating, two years of courting and twenty-one years of marriage, that women do not like to marry broke men. Becoming a good presenter, going from individual sales calls to branch broadcast meetings, made my income jump from $75,000 to over $300,000.

What should you talk about? Speak on the economy, the capital markets, real property trends, public policy or in any area in which you are well-versed, particularly financial areas that the public can relate to and can pass on a message of hope. Give away your financial wisdom for free-no strings attached. Create the experience of what you sell, but do not pitch. Educate first, create a friendly climate.

There are three principles to consider when engaged in public speaking.

The first key principle of success is the **law of compensation**-give in order to get.

The second principle is the **law of increasing returns**-you will get back more than you give out.

The third principle is the **law of delayed gratification**-you will get it back after you give it out.

If you want to succeed as a broker, put these principles of success to work. Duplicate yourself through other people by creating a referral based practice; you cannot expect to get rich anytime soon unless you create a way to duplicate or leverage yourself.

What would you rather have- $500,000 in cash or a penny a day doubled for thirty days? Delayed gratification: a penny a day doubled for 30 days works

out to be over a million dollars. But after 7 days, it is 64 cents!

J. Paul Getty had a simple philosophy and became one of the wealthiest men the world had ever known. Getty would rather have 1% of 100 people's efforts than 100% of one. Surround yourself with ambitious people, cause them to make a great deal of money and don't worry about your reward. Getty understood the Law of Compensation. As you help other people benefit, you are rewarded. Prospects will ask you about your offering, remembering your outreach and kindly gestures.

Some call this educational marketing, I call it cosmic marketing. If you share something of value, it will come back to bless you. The law of reciprocity is irrefutable and biblical.

Cast your bread over running waters. For, after a long time, you shall find it again. *Ecclesiastes 11:1*

Another 'bible' in networking is ***How to Win Friends and Influence People***, written by Dale Carnegie in 1936. Translated into thirty-five languages and with fifteen million copies sold, it is the seminal work on human engineering. Did you know that there are brokers active in the business who do not actually like people? The biggest money makers in our industry are not the smartest, but are great communicators.

Carnegie's book may have been written to enhance social skills, but it is a must read for business because the biggest problem in business is in dealing not with products but with people. The difference to winning at business often comes down to attitude, effort and relationships.

"Serving the needs of others is the only legitimate business today. Get to know the needs of your clients."
–Peter Giannini, founder of Bank of America

Think about clients who have walked out after an extended time of working together. You've given them beautiful service, market-timed their investments to a tee and yet they left. On the flip side, there are clients who stick with you no matter what. Their transactions may have been mediocre or worse, you have hurt them financially and yet they come back for more. You feel sheepish and can't figure out why they haven't left you. You'd leave you, but they remain faithful.

Carnegie claims that 85% of one's income is based off of personality, relate-ability and charisma. The remaining fifteen per cent is technical knowledge. Seventy-five years later, a prominent broker dealer surveyed its affluent clients and found that seventy-one per cent select an advisor with qualities NOT associated with financial knowledge.

The goal is to make people feel better about themselves after they engage you. If you can do that, you will never lose them. Personality and the ability to talk and listen are more important than the knowledge of Latin verbs or a sheepskin from Harvard.

"Be simple in words, manners and gestures. Amuse as well as instruct. If you can make a man laugh, you can make him think and make him like and believe in you." **–Alfred E. Smith, governor of NY, presidential candidate, "FFM Degree" (from the Fulton Fish Market)**

As a side note, if during an appointment someone offers you a beverage, or any other form of hospitality, TAKE IT! They are trying to be gracious and by refusing it, you kill the chemistry. I've seen many sales blown because a broker is on a "diet" or doesn't drink coffee. Do you want to be on the right side or do you want to be rich? I don't care if it is homemade pumpkin pie laced with pet hair, accept the offer.

One of the things that will never change and continue to help build your business are people skills. Being a broker is a people business, not a product or a service business. People grow, products flow. People move products, products don't move people. That's what this thing is all about. I don't make the rules: if you don't like people, you will not be successful.

To be big in this business, you have to lift people higher up than yourself. I used to think that in order to be big, I had to cut people down and I was pretty good at it. I felt superior to people, engaging frequently in little verbal clashes with prospects, and ripping them to shreds with my knowledge. Who really wins in this kind of situation? Was it that important to be right or would I have gained more by doing the right thing? Not only did I possibly lose that one customer-but also, everyone that he or she talked to after that. I learned to leave the door open for everyone's opinion.

***"Keep away from small people who try to belittle your ambitions. Small people always do this, but the really great make you feel that you too, can be great."* –Mark Twain**

The Italian economist, Vilfredo Pareto made the observation that twenty per cent of the population owned eighty per cent of the property in Italy. Later, business-management consultant Joseph Juran made it a principle and found that eighty per cent of the effects come from twenty per cent of the causes. Eighty per cent of most committee work is commonly done by twenty per cent of people. Therefore, you don't need 100 accounts to make you wealthy-just twenty. It is simple- twenty people stand between you and a lifestyle of the top 1%. Twenty relationships, twenty yeses.

Chapter Five

BUILD YOURSELF BEFORE YOU BUILD YOUR BUSINESS

"I know the price of success: dedication, hard work and an unremitting devotion to the things you want to see happen." **–Frank Lloyd Wright**

Psychologists tell us that we have 40,000 thoughts going through our skulls every single day and eight-seven per cent of those thoughts are negative.

Champion brokers know that one attracts the people they are and not necessarily the people they want or need. Television psychology guru Dr. Phil says we teach people how to treat us. It all boils down to self-talk and self-belief. Optimism is like a magnet and a good broker needs to share his optimism with clients.

Your business will never outgrow your self-image-no one is going to feel confident working with a broker who is unsure of himself. I could place ten huge clients with you and they would be gone within a year if you did not have the self-confidence to handle them.

Leaders are readers and readers are leaders.

Successful people in any walk of life are in constant learning mode and naturally curious; know-it-alls are all uniformly broke in spirit. I tell my kids that they will be the same people five years from today except for three things: the places they visit, the people they meet and the books they read.

"I really had a lot of dreams as a kid and I think a great deal of that grew out of the fact that I had a chance to read a lot." –Bill Gates

One way to build confidence is through the knowledge you gain from reading-build yourself a library and you will build your career. Every condominium complex in my home state is dotted with cable lines and satellite dishes; but every five million dollar home has a library. Successful people read every day. Build a 'success library' and read for at least fifteen minutes every day. Reading good positive, success oriented literature is a short cut to learning. Turn your automobile into a classroom-listen at every opportunity and replace negative information in the news with positive, motivational and inspiring messages that will become a part of who you are.

"It is a good thing for an uneducated man to read books of quotations." -Winston Churchill

Brokers sometimes say, "Listen, you don't understand, I am a self-starter-I don't need this motivational stuff," which is equivalent to the guy riding the pine at a football game saying, "I don't need one of those helmet things." He is right, when you are on the bench, you might not think you need the helmet thing. But if you have it on, then you are ready to play, more ready than the guy sitting next to you who is not wearing his.

When you are on the field of life, you need the motivational stuff to be ready. Reading changes your thinking long term.

Attend seminars. A business, professional or personal improvement seminar will both energize and refresh you with new ideas and enhance skills. Surround yourself with interesting people who associate with other positive people. Leaders making the income and having the lifestyle are at these types of meetings, expanding their networking capabilities. Have you ever forced yourself to attend an event that turns out to be an opportunity in disguise? Think the conference is too far away? Inconvenient? Expensive? You will not make it as a broker if you continue to act like a salaried employee, waiting for a paycheck. Success is built on inconvenience and is directed at people open and willing to change.

Otherwise, stay married to the 40X40 Plan-40 hours a week for 40 years. Attend a seminar or stay at home, parked on the La-Z-Boy, marked "L" for loser. I resisted traveling outside of my comfort zone for years and guess how much I was making? Zip, zero, nothing, zilch, goose-egg, nada. In fact, I took it one step further and was actually in the hole financially.

There are only two dragons to feed if you wish to be successful as a broker: enthusiasm and phone calls. Housing starts, unemployment numbers, Kurtosis, trade deficits, Sharpe ratios, twelve month performance or any other silly measurement is inconsequential to your growth.

Compare your first year to this last year in business. Which had great growth? I'll bet it was the first. How can that be? When new, you are at the height of your ignorance and enthusiasm. Compared to last year, you have so much more wisdom, yet business waned. What happened to your initial excitement?

If you want to succeed, you're going to have to get excited and stay excited. Nothing will happen in your life unless somebody gets excited about something and you had better pray it is you. If you cannot get fanatical about something, then you will just stumble through life, getting up day after day, week after week, month after month, year after year, just getting by, existing, not living. Social status does not breed excitement, enthusiasm does.

"Success consists of going from failure to failure without a loss of enthusiasm." **–Winston Churchill**

Discipline: Be as tough on yourself as you are on your kids. If your kids are not making the grade in school, then something's got to give. What gets yanked from the kids-should also be yanked from the broker-the iPad, the iPods, the cell phone (except for business calls of course), TV, snacks, hanging out with friends-you get the point. Why do you do that? Because success is a decision. Decide whether you are going to be successful or a failure. The word decision is Latin for cut off.

Don't let your ego get in the way of your income. Status types in our business know it all, show it all and owe it all. The same people with all of the pride buy expensive homes, take luxury vacations, make exotic foreign purchases-many with the intentions of impressing others. They want to show everyone how well they are doing. However, no one is ever impressed when they see foreclosure signs or the repo man driving away in that fancy car. Friends are not going to stick around and pay your bills. Surround yourself with people who support your dream-it is more important to care about what your wife and family thinks than superficial materialists or status-seekers.

"It is better to hang out with people better than you. Pick out associates whose behavior is better than yours and you'll drift in that direction."
-Warren Buffett

If you want to grow your business, grow yourself. What is your dream? Without a dream, a goal, a reason or a purpose, it's not going to work. Dreams are motivators and without them, chances of succeeding are very slim. It is good to identify the reason to set goals for yourself so that you will not look backwards, but move ahead with all the energy and conviction of a great explorer. Dreams inspire conscious decisions to move ahead.

***"If you can dream it, you can do it."* –Walt Disney**

Sometimes we don't know what it takes to succeed-every single success story of the people mentioned in Chapter Two follow the same pattern of dream-struggle-victory. What started as a dream became an almost tunnel-vision-like struggle, resulting in a phenomenal victory. None of the self-made millionaires and billionaires gave up and remained optimistic that their visions would come to fruition, no matter what it took.

"People are quite remarkable when they start thinking they can do things. When they believe in themselves they have the first secret of success."
- Norman Vincent Peale

In order to succeed, you must visualize your success and then work towards it. You cannot perform with an average effort-you must pull out all of the stops-improve yourself, convince yourself of your mission. Ninety-five per cent of people say they have to see it to believe it, but five per cent act on believing for achieving.

Most people have no comprehension of where they are going. They take a job, wait for raises and eventually wonder what it was all for. Dream big and then go big after those dreams- do not stop at ordinary.

"People without a dream are mentally dead." –Ben Franklin

Do you want financial independence-the ability to pay your bills and not live paycheck to paycheck? You will have to leave the land of the familiar and get uncomfortable.

In life you pay one of two prices; the price of discipline or the price of regret. –Scott Peppard

---

If you had a scale, the price of discipline would weigh ounces and the price of regret would weigh tons. You are going to pay one of the two. Pay the price of discipline based on the size of your dream. Get practical: make a list of the things you have to do, the steps you have to take-expose your offering and always follow through. Become disciplined on the basics of the business and you will never have to pay the price of regret.

Nothing in the world can take the place of persistence. Talent will not; nothing is more common than the unsuccessful man with talent. Genius will not; unrewarded genius is almost a proverb. Education will not; the world is full of educated derelicts. Persistence and determination alone are omnipotent. The slogan "press on" has solved, and will always solve, the problems of the human race." **–Calvin Coolidge**

Your tolerance for discomfort equals your potential for wealth. To become successful, you need to get uncomfortable. Most of life's happiness lies outside of your comfort zone. Just about every significant financial, emotional, and relational breakthrough in your life comes one step beyond a massive upheaval and with it a great deal of pain. You grow the most during uncomfortable times. Don't focus on a comfortable life. Focus on your goals and earn a comfortable life.

***"If you want to make life easy, make life hard."* -Johann Wolfgang von Goethe**

Success comes when you focus on your goals, not on the difficult steps you take to get there. I was looking at the ground when I first started out, devoting my energy to the little or mundane things I had to do to make it as a broker instead of the bigger picture. I would often forget about my dream, allowing negativity to crowd out optimism. Before my income took off, I had to change my thinking. I had to unlearn conventional wisdom. I had to read and learn from successful people who not only talked the talk but more importantly, walked the walk.

***"Live a reality that exceeds your dreams."* –Tom Anderson, co-founder of Myspace**

Most people underuse their abilities inherited at creation. God gave you the most exciting thing in your life, located right between your ears. Yet most people only ask their brains to do what they did the day before, making tasks passive.

My favorite story about breaking mental barriers comes from the animal kingdom.

The city zoo had a bear in a ten foot long cage. They put the food in at one end and the bear at the other. Every day the bear would walk over the ten foot distance, eat, walk back and lay down. The bear did the same thing day after day for ten years, watched by all of those who knew his habits. One day, the keeper removed the cage. The bear entered the platform and walked the same number of steps: ten feet forward to eat, ten feet back to sleep-all in the absence of bars! The next day, the keepers moved the food fifteen feet away instead of the usual ten and guess what? The bear went ten feet and stopped!

People become complacent in life-ten feet forward, ten feet back...

They get up and do the same thing for money today what they got up and did for money yesterday. And they will get up tomorrow and do the same thing they did today. Their lives are going round and round in a circle 100 miles an hour on the road to nowhere without even knowing it. Before you know it they are getting the gold watch or worse yet, the pink slip and it's all over. Ten feet forward, ten feet back. Pointing out that they are in a rut, is often futile, causing them to become defensive and uncomfortable. This discomfort should signal change. If you haven't changed your alarm clock in three years, you are in a rut.

***"Should you find yourself in a chronically leaking boat, energy devoted to changing vessels is likely to be more productive than energy devoted to patching leaks."* –Warren Buffett**

If you think you are sick and tired now, keep doing the same thing for the same pay and guess where you will be in five years? You will be worse off because taxes and inflation will eat you alive!

If you always do what you always did, you will always get what you always got. – Old Saying

The only way to associate with winners is to succeed and the only way to succeed is to associate with winners. Adopt winning habits. Winners and losers are like oil and water-each can only handle about two minutes of advice from the other. **Winners make things happen, losers make excuses.**

"I say there is no darkness but ignorance... oftentimes excusing of a fault doth make the fault worse by excuse." **–William Shakespeare**

Success and money do not care what day of the week it is, or what holiday it is or who has a vacation week coming up. You either make dust or eat dust. There should be a new national holiday called Free Enterprise Day where Americans celebrate work. Winners leave a trail, they don't follow a path (Emerson, paraphrased). When your peers head for the pub on Friday afternoon, you should be turning up the heat. Your prospects will be in a good mood with the weekend coming up and your competition may already be on the road to the beach.

Think: Thank God I'm Free instead of TGIF

I typically write my best business during the month of August and the week of Christmas! I never make my calls on Monday morning-people are nursing hangovers and having angina. (Most heart attacks occur on Monday mornings!)

Have a sense of urgency, but be patient. Not many of us were born to be brokers. Improve yourself, your attitude according to your dream-if you need to change some things in your life, you need to change some things in your life.

***"The height of insanity is continuing the same activity and expecting a different result."* -Albert Einstein, father of modern physics**

Chapter Six

PROSPER IN ANY MARKET

"Things may come to those who wait, but only those things left behind by those who hustle." **–Abraham Lincoln**

Half of all of the Fortune 500 companies began operation during a recession or depression. Think about it. If you are trying to time your success as a broker, would you rather commence operation at the top or bottom of the business cycle? Get in when things are bad! Mature and seasoned business people embrace a downturn. Market stress is supposed to happen-it is inevitable and necessary. Amateurs fall by the wayside while lifers make bigger profits.

Think of a market correction as purgatory, not a punishment.

It is a failure of most to have imagination during a crisis. More often than not, agents, advisors and salesmen make their biggest profits during times of market stress. When brokers in Midtown Manhattan are thinking about jumping out of one story windows, these giants are landing new accounts. They refuse to participate in the orgy of capitulation. They divorce themselves from the static, the noise and negativity that permeate CNBC, the water-cooler herd and the coffee urn gang. (*Gossip destroys a practice-if you complain you remain in your circumstance.)*

***"I don't measure a man's success by how high he climbs, but how high he bounces back when he hits bottom."* –General George S. Patton**

Successful business people know that markets don't crash, they correct. They see the capital market or housing price market not as a wealth loss, but a wealth transfer from owners to buyers.

These are changing times, not hard times.

I hear so many brokers cry that times are tough: "Gotta circle the wagons and cut back." "Job's the new raise... lucky to have one." The hallmarks of loser mentality. It comes down to a mindset.

***"Obstacles are frightful things you see when you take your eyes off the goal."* –Henry Ford**

See it big, keep it simple. Don't cut back, sell out.

Great companies such as Progressive Insurance, Microsoft and Southwest Air do not over expand in good times and don't cut back in bad.

Practice radical restraint-this will protect performance.

"The rich get richer and the poor get poorer." This statement is often true for the reason that prosperous people understand that they have to duplicate and leverage their money and time.

"Recognize that there will be failures, and acknowledge that there will be obstacles. But you will learn from your mistakes and the mistakes of others, for there is really very little learning in success." –Michael Dell

Eliminate the negative by identifying it. If you are a student of the news, you are negative. If you are a student of history, you are positive. The media shouts that America is in a recession, but I refuse to participate. Negative self-talk perpetuates a negative attitude and will hold you back. Determine the difference between the negative and the positive, understand it and echo positive both to yourself and your prospects-there is always a silver lining.

"Flaming enthusiasm, backed by horse sense and persistence is the quality that most frequently makes for success." –Dale Carnegie

This business has everything to do about promotion. You promote your product, your service, your team, your affiliated company, your vendors, your country and of course yourself. Have no shame in your game. If you promote all of these things to everyone, you will have a very big business.

It's not only what you know or who you know, but who knows you.

Without promotion, something terrible happens-NOTHING! Don't shake your ahead and say you know these things unless you are doing them every day. To know and not do is not to know. Wealthy people became successful because they were willing to promote themselves and their values. Broke mentality thinks negatively about selling and promotion.

Marketing is the engine of your business, branding the fuel.

It is always better when someone sells you than when you sell yourself. Don't think of yourself as an agent, broker, advisor or salesperson. Instead, think of yourself as a marketer. With good niche marketing, sales are easy. Marketing eliminates the sales department and branding eliminates the marketing department.

Surround yourself with the people who are excited about their futures. Duplicate their work and identify what it is that you really want. I have witnessed a lot of salespeople talk themselves out of a sale by emphasizing negative information with prospects and clients. Never do this! Whatever you complain about expands and takes on a life of its own. Clients will not commiserate; they will run. You must sell optimism with historical evidence. Act as if. The motto of success is to live in the vision, not the circumstance.

Instead of worrying, work, set goals and commit. Worry is simply a prayer for what you don't want to have happen.

***"The biggest risk is to not take risks."* –Mark Zuckerberg, founder of Facebook**

Chapter Seven

HOW TO BUILD OR REBUILD THE BOOK

"You have to have a fighting spirit. You have to force moves and take chances." **–Bobby Fischer**

Former chairman and CEO of Bank of America, Hugh McColl stated "In business, you either grow or die!" Do not aspire to maintain your business. Stagnation is as good as dead. You cannot maintain a marriage, fitness or a business by doing nothing. Everything is either going forward or backwards, nothing stays the same forever. That is the magical thinking of children not the proactive productiveness of optimistic adults. Treading water gets old.

"Out of sight, out of mind..."

Statistics on client satisfaction reveal that if not contacted once a month, customers perceive it as indifference. You may assume that they will think you are being polite, appreciating the fact that you are not being a pest when in reality, you are becoming invisible. You need to be in love with your people and your work. Establish a real relationship. The opposite of love is not hate-it is indifference. When you love, your heart races. When you hate your heart races. During indifference, the heart flatlines.

Visualize yourself as you appear to both your existing and prospective clients. Are you optimistic? Or are you the bearer of bad news. Are you articulate? How is your grammar? Do you have great information to pass along based on all of that motivational reading you have been doing?

As a broker, you are constantly wordsmithing, painting pictures with what you say, both in person and on the phone. Record your outbound prospecting phone calls. Play them back to someone NOT in the business. If they dry heave or go to sleep, it is time to make a change. Become an artist in grammar and syntax. Conduct postmortem examinations on your prospecting interactions, to improve your manners, pitch, approach and listening skills.

"Never use a long word when a short word will do. Unqualified superlatives are the worst of all. De-accentuate euphemisms. If any word is improper at the end of a sentence, a linking verb is. Avoid trendy locutions that sound flakey. Last but not least, avoid clichés like the plague." **–William Safire**

All professionals spend hours out of the view of other people, whether it is family time, conducting research about their business, putting on the green or in the weight room. What can you do to be memorable in the minds of clients? How do you reinforce relationships and make the difference in the minds of clients so that they are convinced that "you are the one"? Get to know your clients. Know what they like to read, play, vacation, drink and eat. Surprise them with your knowledge of these things by giving information that might be useful. Pass along a newspaper clipping of a restaurant or event they may be interested in. Share a gardening tip, a quote, the title of a good book. Be interested and interesting.

The best place to (re)build your book is to go back into your book. Your wealth is closer to you than you think. Most of us spend so much time, money and energy searching for fortune, achievement and opportunity when most can be found in our own back yards-the resources to achieve all good things are present in one's own community.

You are not writing enough business from your existing clients? When you are first getting started as a broker, you may find that you are the most ambitious person you know, feeling like you have no true friends. Everyone gets off to a shaky start. When I first started selling on commission, I felt like I was giving a disease away. Remember the angst you felt on your first days back at school? It wasn't as much about the end of summer as it was wondering who you would know in your classes.

Successful people are consistent and persistent, despite initial reservations and setbacks. The only thing that will stop you is you. You can overcome any hesitation or fear by persevering with the tasks at hand.

***"Take the first step in faith. You don't have to see the whole staircase, just take the first step."* –Martin Luther King**

You need to know these five things in order to make it:

---

1. What you want and why you want it.
2. What you will sacrifice in order to get what you want and when you expect to have it-set a date
3. Associate with successful, positive, goal-oriented people who are willing to help you achieve your own goals
4. A written plan on how you are going to achieve the goals you set
5. A willingness to work this plan consistently and persistently

---

You can have anything you want. If you can dream it, you can have it. We all start out with dreams, but somewhere along the line, someone knocks us down, admonishing us to be realistic. Stop listening to people who live paycheck to paycheck. You can listen to the wrong people in life and go broke in a hurry. The 40X40 plan does not work. Do you want to work hard for a few years or easy for 40? I did not feel ambitious enough to work for someone else for 40 years...that's ambition! I don't mind working now, if I can be lazy later.

Some will tell you not to set your sights too high to avoid disappointment. Well, what do you accomplish if you set your sights too low? You might be missing the opportunity to "hit it big." Sometimes when we get negative feedback, we think about slipping back to old habits-more sleep, more free time, extending our weekends and being one with the couch. We might rationalize and retreat to a nice, safe job with a steady paycheck. But if freedom is your goal, then wake up.

Try this: Write out a day in your life. What do you want to do when you retire? What time are you going to get up in the morning? Will you eat breakfast at 7AM before a round of golf or will you sleep until noon? If you golfed every day would you get sick of it? And what about the wife? Do you envision being able to send her off on endless shopping sprees without worrying about prices? Would you like to take your family boating or skiing? Write down what you are willing to do today to achieve your dreams.

***"Dreams come true; without that possibility, nature would not incite us to have them."* –John Updike**

Get on a plane, train or an automobile and visit your top twenty-five clients eyeball to eyeball. It costs seven times more to land new clients, then to expand business with existing clients. You need to contact new people at least four times a day and get in front of a new pair of eyeballs. Show your unique selling proposition twenty times a month minimum. You need to do that to get momentum and make things happen. When you expose your offerings only a few times a month, it is difficult to keep the momentum going and to handle rejections. A huge percentage of people who quit the brokerage business, do so before they have received five meaningful rejections.

Have you received five no's yet? Yes? Then you are already 80% of people who are just starting out.

Just fail your way to success!

I mean how many of you had the dream when you were growing up of making 25, 50, 100 calls a day to perfect strangers? Everything refers back to your dream, your goals your reason for doing any of this? Let these thoughts energize your words and actions. After five closing attempts, it is go or forget it. I do not mean to forget prospects as human beings; you just need to concentrate your efforts on others.

And why are you doing all of this? Because **SUCCESS IS A DECISION!**

***"If you can dream it, you can do it."*-Walt Disney**

If you are not making it as a broker, then you need remove things that are getting in the way of your success.

Some of us need a "to don't" list: TV in general, new shows, the weather channel, sports updates, internet surfing, certain people in your life, meaningless conversation, gossip and all negative thoughts. Every night, 98% of people are inputting negativity into their lives via the television; practicing for the future in front of the idiot box. You'll be surprised how much you can accomplish when the energy wasters are eliminated.

***"A pessimist sees the difficulty in every opportunity; the optimist sees the opportunity in every difficulty."* -Winston Churchill**

There are a number of electronic devices in your home or office. One multiplies your income, several divide it. I am not going to state the obvious, but here's a hint: did you know that the strongest muscle in every American male is his right thumb-the one that works the remote control.

Make a decision whether you are going to make it as a broker. If you have not made a decision to make it, you have made an automatic decision not to make it. No action equals failure. Success begins with a decision that something is going to happen. You don't need to know how you are going to get something done before you begin to do it. When you confuse the decision with the how-to process, you won't end up making a decision. This is called decision constipation.

"The only thing that stands between a man and what he wants from life is often merely the will to try and the faith to believe it is possible."
–Richard M. DeVos

If you cannot see something before you have it, you will never have it. Sometimes we wait for someone to show us how to succeed, rather than making a conscious decision to success and finding a way. A winner just needs to know it can be done. When you know who you are, what you want and how to get it, no one can stop you, except yourself.

***"So many people can be responsible for your success, but only you are responsible for your failure."*-Unknown**

Everyone wants success, but few are willing to commit. There are three levels of commitment-where do you fit in?

---

1. I'll try
2. I'll do my best
3. I'll do whatever it takes (so long as it is legal, ethical and moral)

Only those who commit at the third level will achieve success. American immigrants are four times as likely to become millionaires as those born in the US; they understand the value of doing whatever it takes.

In order to make it as a broker, you have to keep growing. School is never out for professionals and if you are only as good today as you were yesterday, then you are going backwards. You cannot create something greater than what you are; you cannot give something you don't have. You have two income aspects: brain and body. Which do you feed the most? You are worth $7.50 from the neck down but multiple millions from the neck up. FEED THE BRAIN. Keep learning to grow as a broker and share that knowledge with your clients. If you put nothing into your brain, nothing will flow out of your mouth.

"Your brain is much better than you think; just use it."
-Leonardo da Vinci

Chapter Eight

WHERE AND HOW TO FIND CLIENTS

"The secret to getting ahead is getting started." –Agatha Christie

Most people are starving in three areas of their life: relationships, time and money. You can help all three if you think strategically about what you do for a living.

As discussed in Chapter Six, clients can easily be found within walking distance of your home, church, synagogue, school, community centers, local organizations, even on line at a grocery store-any place where people gather is a place for you to network. In any market, there is the potential for an overlooked marketplace. One need not look elsewhere for the opportunity to achieve one's dreams-dance with the ones who brought you.

Behind every successful spouse may be another successful spouse; each with their own lists of contacts. The more organizations you join, the more people you get to know, the more opportunities to prove yourself as a private citizen and a professional. Being an active part of your community is not only the right thing to do, but it adds credibility to your image as a trustworthy person to whom contacts may run to for advice and eventual sales. Think about the people you grew up with and those who were admired by you, your family and other members of your town. They probably were the ones with the highest standards and values, the married men who wore their wedding bands proudly, the men who made time for their families, the people who pitched in whenever or wherever they could. These same people were those that many looked up to and believed in. Model yourself after those same kinds of people who were coincidentally successful, perhaps your mentors.

"80% of success is showing up." –Woody Allen

How do you make contacts with clients? How do you bridge the gap between friendship and business?

There are certain nasty words in our profession and you must strive to reverse the image to a more professional, profitable and long-lasting relationship.

1. **The 'Referral'**. Amateurs ask for referrals, pros earn them. If you are that good, people will promote you. Talk to the many to find the few. And the few you find will talk to the many-that's when it gets fun! Those are called referrals!
2. The **'Introduction'**. The problem with asking for a referral is that you put people on

the hook, possibly leveraging a relationship. Introduction is preferred and works 60% of the time, whereas a referral is effective only 20% of the time.

3. The **'Commission'**. When hearing the word commission, I automatically think of what I coulda/woulda/shoulda get for free. Use the words "fee for service" in lieu of commission.
4. The **'Competition'**. Don't de-edify your competitors nor should you edify them either. Your offering is the crème de la crème in the area of service, quality, resources and legacy. Everyone else is…the industry standard.
5. The **'Appointment'**. When I hear the word appointment, I think of three hour root canals. Use the word visit instead.

***"You only have to do a few things right in life so long as you don't do too many things wrong."*-Warren Buffett**

Ok, so we have this new vocabulary and we have joined a bunch of community organizations, but HOW do we find the clients?

Everyone is sitting on a goldmine-a potential data-base of clients.

First of all do not consider your data base as a mailing list, but a list of relationships. Many brokers work off an Excel spreadsheet, a Rolodex, Outlook, Christmas card/wedding lists, DayTimer/planner, directories. I am advocating that you centralize your data base and make it a living, breathing document. When you begin to think of these names as real people, they will become relationships that are meaningful as well as potentially profitable.

The Internet-With the Internet, there is no such thing as a cold call-it's almost like cheating. Every yahoo has a Yahoo factor. Before phoning any prospect, you could turn a list of unknowns into common threads just by doing a little profiling. The idea is to make cold leads warm, warm leads hot, hot leads red hot, red hot leads white hot. Out of 100 names from a phone book, you can turn common ground with 20. Bring up those common threads within the first few moments of the call.

"Push through the pain, and conquer the obstacles. Regardless of what you think today, it won't matter five years from now. So don't be afraid." **-unknown**

Attend trade associations-not yours, your customers! To be successful, observe or extract systems, procedures, processes and thinking that you can use in your practice. That is, take filaments of non-related industries, combine into hybrids and import into your business.

Get stupid again; zero-base your thinking. Someone once said, unlearn most of what you know, and then become capable of rational thought. Unlearn most of what got you where you are. What got you to the Promised Land will not get you into the Promised Land. Ask yourself, "If I were to do it all over again, how would I do it?" Now go ahead and do that! What got you to your current income level, will not get you to your next income level. It is about suspending your own anal status quo thinking.

Your customers don't want your stuff, they want profit. The state of their business is an indicator of yours. The secondary benefit of attending outside trade associations is learning your pre-retirees mission, vehicle, vocation.

SHARE A PROFITABLE IDEA PICKED UP AND THEY WILL NEVER LEAVE YOU. Attending your top five client's trade associations will give you a better understanding of them-you may even hear something and can share it. Sound ridiculous? Significant advancements in industries often come from outsiders. Albert Einstein was a mathematician. Ben Franklin was an apprenticed printer who became known for scientific discoveries. Darwin was considered the greatest naturalist of all time, but was educated as a geologist.

***"Share your success and help others succeed. Give everyone a piece of the pie. If the pie's not big enough, make a bigger pie."* –Dave Thomas**

Sometimes you are too close to the problem in an industry and you need a fresh perspective. I'm often reminded of Arthur Jones, inventor of Nautilus Fitness Machines: "To become proficient in any endeavor, seek out the expert in that field and do the exact opposite!" Makes one stop and ponder.

NETWORKING GROUPS: Most of these groups are too big and full of other salespeople; each member is a carbon copy of the other—financial advisor, attorney, accountant, estate planner, etc. They are too congruent. The best "swap meets" for leads are self-organized, of six people or less and composed of professionals with common clientele but uncommon vocations. Compatible but not competitive groups such as personal trainer/wellness instructor, plastic surgeon/pastor, landscaper/architect, realtor, luxury cars sales/leasing or travel agent.

You might be thinking, they've got no money and I am not going to waste my time. Often the people you least suspect may very well lead you to a winner. It is not who YOU know, but often who other people know.

Most brokers do not actively prospect for clients and those who do sometimes have no idea about what they are doing. On top of their lists of potentials are accountants, doctors, lawyers-those assumed to have investable assets and who may be easier to contact by phone. But the average broker is not a CPA, never went to medical school or sat for the bar. They have no common ground. Accountants, doctors and attorneys have money, but not real money.

According to millionaire aficionado Thomas Stanley, the biggest concentrations of wealth in the United States are found amongst owner operators of boring industries. Vending machine merchants, dry cleaners, mobile home park owners, et cetera and are of Russian, Scottish and Hungarian descent. You are better off prospecting in a community you are familiar with-prior occupations and/

or hobbies. What group of personal injury law, medicine, transportation, catering, faith, do you have the strongest connections with?

Be relatable and your prospects will be more receptive. People do not like being called off as list, checked off as you scroll downward. You need to make every approach with an air of exclusivity.

Try this: Counsel with someone in the community and ask, "Do you have a few minutes to give some advice? I enjoy working in the ______community, but I am not sure where all the money is. If you were me, how would you get to know the people with the dollars?" Of course some would say that is crass, but the bottom line is the bottom line, and ask in any way you feel comfortable and of course, respectful, but ask!

One client of mine is doing a bang-up job prospecting and landing the accounts of restaurants. Why? He used to own a bar back in the 80's and understands the problems and headaches associated with owning a restaurant.

If you are involved in the coaching or teaching of young people, you have a fantastic opportunity to find clients and expand your base. I have a client that leads Boy Scouts, teaches CCD and coaches lacrosse. Every season each student receives a dossier, and a bio on this instructor: where he grew up, his family, where he lives and oh yeah, what he does for a living. Brilliant! And trust me, parents approach him. You **remove the aspect of**

leveraging relationships or soliciting business and make yourself a magnet of approachability.

There are countless ways to find clients that I outline in my individual coaching sessions. The idea is to get the creative juices flowing exponentially and you will come up with your own brilliant ideas.

You are one phone call, one relationship away from an explosion. It happens so often. A broker may be treading water with a tiny life preserver-his former way of looking at his business prospects-his itty bitty practice and then BANG! He hits pay dirt by landing one account that refers him to another and then another and then it begins to cascade from there.

***"I think the harder you work the more luck you have. Hard work is good for the soul. And it keeps you from feeling sorry for yourself because you don't have time."*- Dave Thomas, billionaire founder of Wendy's**

Chapter Nine

MAKE MORE, WORK LESS

"There is no such thing as a good tax." –Winston Churchill

No matter how good you are at what you do, there is one thing that will wipe you out: **the progressive income tax**-work harder to have less. Most employees have two sources of income-gross and net. Who did all of the work to generate the gross? The employee. Who gets all of the difference? Uncle Sam does. The average American pays 42 cents in some form of tax on every dollar.

I love asking salaried people what they make. They will always state their gross income; they are afraid to tell you what they are clearing which is the net. Most employees work through the month of May before any of their hard-earned money stays in their homes.

In 1965, one in seventeen people worked for the government; in 1970, one in eleven worked for the government and according to current statistics-one in six people currently work for the government! That is an astounding amount! Who pays their salary? Tax dollars! When the government pays your salary, you do what the government tells you to do. If you really want to live like that, catch a plane to one of the five remaining communist countries. Take your pick. There is China, Cuba, Laos, North Korea or Vietnam.

The only way you will overcome income taxes is through the law. It is extremely difficult to build wealth when the tax man is grabbing half of what you earn. If you are a salaried or hourly wage earner, ask your employer to be paid on performance. Offer your employer the option to exchange your job for a "contract" position. Better yet, work for yourself.

Start your own business, work on commission, get a percentage of revenue/company profits and or stock options. Successful people work for themselves. They do not let someone pick their pockets.

***"You must do the action necessary to achieve the lifestyle you wish to have."* –Tom Anderson, co-founder of Myspace**

Poor people trade their time for money. The problem with this strategy is that your time is limited and by default this philosophy creates an income ceiling that excludes true wealth. That is why non-equity partners in the legal, accounting and healthcare profession make a moderate living. This paycheck to paycheck style of living creates stress and is a good way to die early; at least 36% of employees suffer from premature deaths due to coronaries directly related to stress.

If you trade hours for dollars, it will wipe you out physically, financially and emotionally. Work smart and put time to work for you.

You can make money in one of two ways:

1. **Investments**-putting your money someplace where it will grow. There are certain drawbacks-you need front end capital that is over and above what you need to live on. There is also a degree of risk involved in losing it.
2. **The traditional way**-doing what our educational system teaches us: receive knowledge, education, and experience and ply it for paycheck. If this is how you make your money, you will never succeed because a) you will limit yourself to your own ability and b) you are limited to 24 hour in a day.

Conversely, if you own your own business, or function as an independent contractor, you can legitimately write off half of your lifestyle. How would your lifestyle change if you could take 42% of your income and put it right back into your lifestyle?

If you don't spend it, you pay tax on it. Vehicle, meals, travel, education and a portion of your mortgage in the form of a home office are deductible. That is why you should go first class when travelling for business!

Successful vehicles are camouflaged. Being a broker, agent, advisor or commissioned salesperson builds the American system rather than tearing it down. Understand that even though you may work under a company's "shingle" as a broker or in any other un-salaried position, you are essentially self-employed. Becoming successful in your own business is the greatest thing you can do for yourself, your family and country.

Part of the struggle is that people do not really understand what it means to be the boss. In a business, you need to invest your own time and money before you see any returns. But if you are willing to work hard, the initial investment will far exceed what you will lose as a salaried employee-the freedom to make decisions and to earn an unlimited income for the benefit of you and your family.

***"I have always had a will to succeed, to win, however you phrase it."* –Jack Kent Cooke, billionaire media mogul, owner Washington Redskins**

Another way to earn more by working less is a secret process call outsourcing. This can be in the form of actual people or electronic sources called virtual assistants or VA's for short. Take everything that is mundane off of your plate: emailing, scheduling, phone-calling, and expense reports to name a few. CEO's do not perform these $10/hour type duties. You need to be the idea person, so take the time to train someone and outsource. Your time is best spent on tasks that provide the most benefit-those that bring in the dollars. There are only two things that you cannot outsource: relationships and control over money.

Bring in your outsourcers as freelancers, not employees. You will not be responsible for taxes, insurance or benefits. Many tasks can be completed with technology or computerized programs. You do not have to know how to do everything and should find an assistant to fill in the gaps-to work on your to-do wish list of tasks that would otherwise eat into sales time. Farm out incidental chores.

A VA or other assistant can help improve your productivity. Many VA's become experts at whatever tasks you hire them for and can provide essential feedback on various aspects of your business. As an impartial witness, their input is a result of "fresh eyes" and can be instrumental in streamlining your efforts or coming up with unique strategies; VA's represent the concept of "working on your business", not in it.

An additional perk of training the right VA is the ability to become less indispensable, therefore gaining the ability to take more time off. This in a sense helps to "monetize" the business-earn more, work less! Although many times, you may feel that it is hard to give up control or you think you can do a better job yourself, it is essential to remain the idea person and delegate repetitive tasks to a detail oriented person.

In order to grow your business, you have to stop doing everything yourself. Be strategic with your time. When you first wake up, have one task at hand-be specific and avoid just going along with any old thing that crops up. Be proactive not reactive. Make a plan to improve your brand by writing a book and promoting yourself via publicity such as speaking to an organization.

***"As much as you need a strong personality to build a business from scratch, you also must understand the art of delegation. I have to be good at helping people run the individual businesses and I have to be willing to step back. The company must be set up so that it can run without me."* –Richard Branson**

Don't be afraid to seek counseling. Every successful person has heroes, models and mentors. In many success stories, someone believed in those people, before they believed in themselves. Oftentimes, these same people are happy to pass on wisdom, ideas, ways they learned from their own mistakes. The very best leaders, athletes and corporate rainmakers have engaged in coaches.

Learn from the experts. They know how to put the fundamentals in order of execution; knowledge in the proper sequence like the alphabet or a cake recipe. It is beneficial to model after successful people—to bounce ideas off of the kinds of people who are where you want to be. Set your sights high and avoid listening to the often misleading advice of the unsuccessful.

If you think you know what you are doing wrong, your counselor does too. Your advocate can pinpoint the areas that may be weak while emphasizing strengths. It is critical to determine factors that may be holding you back, or possibly something simple that you may be overlooking. A counseling session with someone who has already been down that road will help uncover problems and solutions for remedying situations. Pouring efforts into something that isn't working is a waste of time and resources-it is better to consult an expert familiar with your business circumstances.

"Success is a lousy teacher." **–Bill Gates**

A common cause of failure in business is the habit of quitting when one experiences temporary defeats. If you are pursuing a worthwhile dream, always seek the advice of expert council before giving up. While it is beneficial to listen to motivational material to keep a positive attitude, the material is not intended as a substitute for a bona fide expert in a given field. A local member of the community, one who is well respected and well known is a much better source of information than a boxed set of audios and videos from a late night infomercial-take it from me! Much of that type of preaching and hype is meant to be delivered to a crowd and very unlikely to be said face to face.

"Don't be afraid to fail. Get out there and experiment and learn and fail and get a rate based on the experiences you have. Go for it and when you go for it, you will know what you are capable of, what the potential is, where the opportunities are, but you can't be afraid to fail because that's when you learn." **–Michael Dell**

A final goal of owning a business is to sell that business. Perhaps you have worked at it and have something profitable to sell. Maybe you have done what you could with it and are ready for another challenge. Or hopefully, you have become so successful that you want to pursue other dreams. There is nothing to say that you cannot sell when the time is right and only you will know the where and when.

***"For me, businesses are like buses. You stand on the corner and don't like where the first bus is going? Wait ten minutes and take another. Don't like that one? They'll just keep coming. There's no end to businesses or buses."* –Sheldon Adelson, billionaire casino owner**

Chapter Ten

CUT THROUGH THE NOISE TO GET NOTICED

***"Good manners come from petty sacrifices."* Ralph Waldo Emerson, American Philosopher**

Salespeople lose millions of dollars every year because of a lack of professionalism and good manners. First impressions DO count and the way you look, the way you speak and even the way you address potential clients speaks volumes.

If you are out of shape, start a fitness regime. If your clothes look rumpled, find a new dry cleaner. If your correspondence is misspelled or grammatically incorrect, take a class in business writing.

And always, always know the proper pronunciation of someone's full name. It takes a long time to build up a relationship-do not insult you customers by being overly familiar from the start. Make sure to always address clients by their surnames. When a telemarketer calls me at home and addresses me as Scott, I am not interested; but if he addresses me as Mr. Peppard, no matter what the circumstances, I will listen. The more difficult the name to pronounce, the better. According to Dale Carnegie, the sweetest sound to any man is that of his own name.

"To recall a voter's name is statesmanship, to forget is oblivion."
-James Farley, United States Postmaster General, 1933-1940

No one cares about who you are, your title or the firm you represent. How do I know that? Can you guess the most popular word in the King's English? (HINT: it is a personal pronoun.) It is the word "I." Everyone is tuned to WIFM or "what's in it for me." They don't care about you! I am always telling my three children "Kids, from the world's perspective, you are special, but not that important."

That being said, there is a sequence of delivery when calling prospects:

1. Personal title surname
2. The referrer's name
3. The message
4. Your name

How you introduce yourself is critical. It is not the words you say, but the music you play. Think Ian Fleming's 007: "Bond, James Bond." Speak, clearly and confidently: "This is George, George Costanza." Why? The receiver is more apt to remember your first name than last and is likely to listen.

***"When you greet someone, look them in the eye and say their name. It is a sign of respect."* –Dave Thomas**

There is also a code of etiquette with regard to email correspondence. When emailing clients or prospects put their name in the subject line; they are more apt to read it. Remember Carnegie's advice that a person's name is the sweetest, most important and recognizable sound in any language. If you send an attachment (pdf, word doc, etc.) save it in their name; they will open it.

The goal is to be professional but slightly unorthodox. Eliminate disingenuous ice breakers such as "How are you?" "Good Morning!" "How's it going?" Icebreakers are for ships, not salespeople.

***"Tell me what you want in the fewest words possible."* –Abraham Lincoln**

If it is good enough for honest Abe, it is good enough for all of us.

Eliminate clichés and redundancies such as "Ya know what I'm saying?" "Ya know what I mean?" "At the end of the day." "It is what it is." I'll bet you can come up with a list of your own of overly used words and phrases that come and go like fashion. Stay away from trendy or dated language. Get a Thesaurus and clean up your act. Use glamour words-commonly known but uncommonly used vernacular.

***"...be the uncommon man."* –Theodore Roosevelt**

When at the opera, symphony or ballet and asked what you do for a living, don't give them the party line -i.e., I am a realtor, financial advisor, etc. You will suck the oxygen right out of the room and the temperature will go to zero. It is a conversation killer, a "feature." Amateurs sell features, professionals sell benefits.

The following examples come from highly successful brokers with billions of dollars under their control.

"I specialize in 401(k) repair strategies."
"I help people avoid foreclosure."
"I teach creative financing to help people purchase a larger home than imagined."
"I educate employees on IRA rollovers."
"I help people who have cashed out as company owners."
"I teach how and when to exercise stock options."

No "F" words (features). You are talking with prospects that are many times the salt of the earth, middle class people with six and seven figures of potential retirement money to invest. Do you think they will get excited with the passé statement: "I manage portfolio risk."

Develop a cocktail commercial that rolls off the tongue and fits your personality. Simple good; complex bad. Come up with a marketing statement, a mission statement that consists of ten words or less that is simple enough to not only be remembered by John Q. Public, but, repeated by referrals! This creates "apostles" for your cause.

It is not simply who you know, it is who other people may know.

Who is more likely to get face time with a prospect?

"Mr. Johnson, would you like to schedule an appointment to have your financial statement reviewed?"

Or

"Mr. Johnson, my team at Acme specializes in showing Verizon employees when and how to exercise their stock options. Would you like us to share some ideas?"

"No man has the right to dictate what other men should perceive, create or produce, but all should be encouraged to reveal themselves, their perceptions and to build confidence in the creative spirit." –Ansel Adams, photographer

I hope by now you realize that the crux of success as a broker, that the dominant determinate is attitude. Getting noticed is more attitudinal than wisdom. Clients in all industries look to their broker for faith. Faith in markets. Faith in our system. Faith in America. Faith in your leadership to guide them through and more importantly that things are not as bad as they appear.

"You earn your reputation by the things you do every day." –Dave Thomas

The path of financial history is on the upturn. Most people slept through tenth grade civics and need to be reminded that this republic is 230 years of correct decisions. We are blessed and bullet-proofed. It is not rational thinking to look to the government for a bailout.

Sales is the bailout. You have to be your own bailout. Focus on your economy, not "the economy".

"Most of us have no imagination during a crisis." **-S.P.**

Markets correct and things do get better. There is more good news than bad news.

The best is yet to come. The rest is up to you. Take action today. Not Monday, not the first of the year. Live your future in the moment. This moment. Are you going to do what is comfortable or what is necessary? You must always do what is necessary.

"Start doing what is necessary; then do what's possible; and suddenly you are doing the impossible." **–Saint Francis of Assisi**

Life gives you lots of opportunity to do what is comfortable. You can do just enough to get by, you know, just enough to make your quota, pay the bills, keep your job. There are plenty of people in the world who do that. In doing so, you will never discover your brilliance.

"Even the greatest was once a beginner. Don't be afraid to take the first step." **-Unknown**

Your genius is not if you are smart. It is HOW you are smart. Everyone has some brilliant moments, but do they sustain them enough to make a difference in their lives. The only way to discover your potential is to go beyond what is comfortable and to do whatever is necessary. Do you want to set your alarm clock to go off at the same time every day? Do you want to drag yourself out of bed to go punch a clock for a minimal paycheck? Do you want to spend the best years of your life making someone else rich? To make it in life, go into business and learn how to work smart. Understand the principles of success and make a decision to succeed.

Whatever you decide to do, make sure to include the element of fun, strive to make money and make a difference. Get involved in civic activities in your community-be an active member with a passion that is infectious and will draw others to follow.

"Do not follow a path, leave a trail."
–Ralph Waldo Emerson

Remember your dream. Practice everything you preach. Rise above the crowd. Make a conscious decision, decide to succeed. There is only room for one dream in any business and if you are working for someone else, you are building someone else's dream. Take hold of your future and work towards your own dream. If you serve to the classes, you will live with the masses. If you focus on your dream and do whatever is necessary to achieve your goals, you will serve the masses and live with the classes otherwise it is back to the plantation.

Let your actions speak louder than words-so loudly that no one will be able to refuse your offers. Take heed dreamers, you have lived the worse day in your life, financially. Dream your way to success. Get started and don't look back.

"A great leader is one who practices what they preach. They lead by example, and create a sense of loyalty and teamwork and are active in their community, sharing their success with those in need." **–Dave Thomas**

"There is one quality that one must possess to win and that is definiteness of purpose, the knowledge of what one wants and a burning desire to possess it." **–Napoleon Hill**

"The way to get started is to quit talking and start doing."**-Walt Disney**

Bonus Ideas

1. Get 10 new pre-qualified referrals now with the **Retirement Celebration.** According to AARP, in 2011 the first of the 'Baby Boom' generation reached what used to be known as the retirement age. For the next 18 years boomers will be turning 65 at a rate of about 8,000 a day; as a result there will be a colossal demand for estate and retirement planning. Phone all of your pre-retirees on the cusp of their last day at work. Have a Retirement Party for clients turning 65! "Dan, we want to celebrate your retirement. We are going to have a luncheon at ___________. Bring ten of your best friends-we will provide transportation as well." Hire a stretch limo and chauffeur him to the banquet you have arranged. This demonstrates to Dan you care and will reward your generosity with ten pre-qualified leads.
2. **Memorex Technique-** I have always been a fan of leaving an enthusiastic voice message for prospects: It is more powerful than an email, in some cases easier to communicate positively than an actual conversation, and you can bypass the "gatekeeper." **Simply record your pitch** and leave it on your

prospect's voicemail. By scripting a well-crafted voicemail, **you can duplicate your enthusiasm over and over again. You are capturing lightning in a bottle!**

3. **A Customer Relationship Management strategy (CRM)** is a low cost technology to find/contact/keep customers. A good CRM system will improve client experience by managing it. This translates into loyalty as it organizes your business, tracks more prospects, helps to close more sales, retains more customers, personalizes email blasts etc. **CRM not only keeps track of your customers, leads and opportunities but helps drive new revenue for your business by client conversation and retention.** It also helps to keep operational costs down. By streamlining your tasks and workflow, you spend less time on manual processes and can focus on the projects that directly affect the bottom line. **You will experience a revolutionary sales impact-** Through a new targeted and efficient selling system you will connect and convert **more clients in less time.** A CRM helps you effectively **leverage technology to increase sales**. I mentioned earlier in the book that **it costs seven times more to land a new client than to expand business with**

existing clients. Therefore retention is more important than acquisition. There are a number of great suppliers available: SAP, Oracle, Salesforce.com, Microsoft CRM, Amdocs and BigContacts. Moving to a full blown CRM system from a rolodex or excel spreadsheet will provide efficient work flow and improve client experience.

4. **The Sample Simple Business Plan that works:** a basic outline for a much needed plan of action

    a. Analysis-break down the complex into bite-sized pieces
    b. Annual sales goals
    c. Top 30 prospect list
    d. Strategies-your plan of action
    e. Weekly activity objectives
    f. Challenges, contingency and exit
    g. Call rotation
    h. Personal Development Plans
    i. Budget

***"Twenty years from now you will be more disappointed by the things you didn't do than by the ones you did do. So throw off the bowlines, sail away from the safe harbor. Catch the trade winds in your "sales."* –**

Mark Twain